The Fast Way to sta

Car Detailing Business

Learn the most effective way too easily and quickly

start a car detailing business in the next 7 days!

Bernard Savage

Content

Chapter 1

Chapter 2

Chapter 3

Chapter 4

Chapter 1

How to easily start a car detailing business;

Start your own auto detailing business or a vehicle detailing service by using our information gathered from over 22 years being in the detailing industry.

If you have been thinking about starting a detailing business, this book will give you all the information for waxing, and detailing vehicles start up tips!

Did you know vehicle detailing professionals can easily earn in excess of $450.00 + a day?

Starting a vehicle detailing business of your own is one of the easiest of all small businesses to start. And the vehicle detailing industry is a "billion dollar business"! The initial start-up costs are well within your reach, and the margin of profit ratio very high!

Vehicle detailing is an easy business to operate, and yet one that will always be necessary, as long as people drive car or trucks. It has a very high rating on all business stability charts, and once started, your detailing business will grow quickly and begin making a considerable amount of money.

When you own your detailing business, there will be no more punching a time clock, working somewhere or for someone you really don't like, and working hard for someone else just so they can earn all of the money. And best of all, the personal satisfaction you will gain from being successful and turning nothing into something. All it takes to be successful in any business is the will and determination.

First of all, you will need to decide exactly what you want the business to be. You can either have a small one man detailing business, or grow it into one with multiple employees and mobile detailing vans, or even, someday become the biggest detailing businesses nationwide! There is no limit to what you can do!

You will need to decide if you want to start it full time or begin slowly by working part time. If you have the funds to go out and buy all the equipment for a start-up detail business, or to start small and slowly build up the funds to buy more and bigger and better equipment, do what fits your situation.

Before starting a vehicle detailing business, gain experience in car detailing by working as an employee or apprentice for an auto detailing company. This experience provides you with customer service skills, the knowledge of how to detail different types of vehicles, and how to run your own business. A successful vehicle detailing business should provide quality care and offer services, such as wash and waxing cars, removing oil from motors, and detailing tires.

Create a business plan to help you stay focused during each stage of business development. Divide your plan into four or five sections. Include information about the types of detail services you plan to provide in the first section. Focus on detailing cars, trucks, or vans, depending on your interest and skills. Additional services include recreational vehicles, motorcycles, limousine, boats or airplanes. Provide a list of detailing equipment and supplies needed to run your business in the second section and include the cost of these items. Outline day-to-day expenses, such as phone, Internet, transportation, and employee costs in the third section. Describe how you plan to market your detailing business in the fourth section. Estimate how much you plan to earn in your first year of business in the fifth section.

You should choose a location for your business. If you plan to work from home, create a space for an office to receive calls, store equipment, complete bookkeeping duties, and store files. Contact local commercial real estate agents to inquire about leasing a space for your business.

Purchase business insurance such as general liability, workers' compensation if hiring employees, product insurance, or home-based business insurance to protect business assets in the event of a lawsuit or settlement. Worker's compensation insurance covers employee accident or injury when on the job. You may also need to purchase a surety bond. A surety bond helps promote an honest relationship between business owner and customer. In the event of a lawsuit or settlement, the state of Kentucky may use the bond to pay for legal expenses.

Apply for a business license by contacting the

Fayette County Clerk's Office, if opening a detailing business in Lexington, or the county clerk's office that serves the county where you want to conduct business. Contact the Kentucky Secretary of State Office to register your business, if forming a corporation, limited liability company, or partnership.

Chapter 2

Simple way to get a Business License:

If you're trying starting a home based auto detailing business, in most counties you must have a business license. It is the law. If you try to run a business without a business license, you will be fined or, in some counties, arrested.

Do you need insurance to get an auto detailing license? If you're operating a detailing business in Fayette County, Kentucky, you don't need insurance to get a license. Different states and counties have their own laws when it comes in regard to license and insurance. In order to find out what's needed in your county, call the County Clerk's office. They will tell you what you'll need to do.

First, decide what you want to name your business. Look for something snappy and easy to remember. I have put together a few names to give you an idea. You are welcome to use any name but be sure no one else is using the names in your state. Check with the County Clerk's office.

*Bright & Shine Detail   * Master Buffer

*Nice-n-Clean   * Hot Wax Detailing

*Red Hot Detailers   * Detailing Experts

* Detailing Masters   *Your Car's Day Spa

*It's A Family Affair Detailing

Some home businesses believe if their company has a professional name, it will help them get more clients. I disagree. It doesn't matter what you call your business. If you follow the plan in this book, your business will be successful.

This is what I did. I wrote down several names for my mobile detailing business. Next, I talked to several friends, asking them what service sounds more professional and which name caught their attention.

That's what you're looking for a name that captures the client's attention.

Once you come up with the name, call your local Commissioner of Revenue Office, which is located in the County Clerk's office in the county governments building. They will help you get a business license. They'll need to know what business you will be running and your business address. You must live in the county where your mobile detailing business is located.

If you go to another county and pick-up customers, you may have to pay a county tax for that area. Once again, contract the County Clerk's office to find out the laws.

This is how it works. If you live in Fayette County but you start pick-up accounts in Franklin County, 12 miles down the road, Franklin's Commissioner of Revenue Office may want their 4.5% annual taxes for you doing business in their County. I know it sucks, but it is the law. I would rather pay $30 to

$50 per year in county taxes than to be fined $300 to $500 for not paying taxes.

Some Counties may check the Zoning Department to make sure your residence is zoned for a mobile detailing business. I have never heard of a county refusing to give license to a mobile detailing business unless you have a fleet of vehicles and a 20 mean operation. If that was the case, you wouldn't need this book, you would be writing one.

Will you need a Tax ID Number? I don't think so. If a man is going to hire you to detail his 1959 Dodge, I don't think he'll be worry about a Tax ID Number. He'll want his car detailed.

Do you have employees or plan on hiring someone in the next few weeks? I wouldn't think about hire anyone until I have more business the I can handle. Once that happens, I will hire someone part-time. When you're hiring full-time employees, it's time to get your Tax Id Number, Social Security, and Worker's Compensation insurance.

Do I need Worker's Compensation Insurance? If you hiring employees, yes. If your employee dings or dents a vehicle when detailing it, you will need insurance for protection.

"Google" Worker's Compensation Insurance. It will direct you to several sites where you can find a list of agents in your area.

Do you need liability insurance to start a car detailing business? In the state of Kentucky, you do not need liability insurance to get license. But I would check my Commissioner of Revenue Office to be on the safe side. If they do request liability insurance, I would work alone until I have the money to get the correct insurance.

This is my opinion. If an employee damages a car, I don't have $2000 to $8000 + to pay a customer for car repairs. It will shut my business down before I get the doors open. Get the insurance and keep it as long as you're in business.

The reason for liability insurance is to protect your business just in case something, like an employee damaging a car, happens. But that's my opinion. It's it left up to you.

Chapter 3

The best way to start your business!

Now you have your business license and insurance, next is the location.

Most small mobile auto detailing businesses do not have an office because they go to their customer's homes to detail their vehicle. The only thing you'll need is a phone to take calls, and detailing equipment and supplies.

If you have a lot of supplies, you will need a spare room. Or, basement would be perfect. Some place you can clean out put down an in-door; -out-door carpet. This room or rooms should be clean and smoke free.

It's my opinion that if you are a smoker, doesn't smoke in a confined room with the equipment.

Wait until you leave the room. I'm not trying to rag on you if you're a smoker, that's your business. But there are people who don't want their vehicle smelling like cigarette smoke. But if you are a smoker, make sure the area where you keep the supplies and tools is smoke free.

Keep a report on every vehicle you detail. This will tell you the date of service, what the customer wanted, condition of the vehicle, what you did, and how much it cost. The customers know their vehicle. They are the boss. Do what they tell you, when they tell you, and you will have a happy client. If a customer requests a car wash with no waxing don't try to talk them into a complete detailing just to run up their bill. Wash the car, have the customer signs your receipt, and move on to the next job. Be honest, giving them what they pay for and thanking them for the business, and move on the next job.

You are professional. Make daily notes on every job. This is very important which is why I'm saying it again. If you purchase a special wax because your client requested it, get two receipts one for you and the one the customer.

If you see any marks, dings, or dents on the vehicle, call the owner right away. Take pictures, record the time, date, and anything the owner says, and keep it in your files. If you have a witness, gets a statement from them about what they saw.

Get the statement in writing and put it in your files. When the owner pays you for your work, have them sign a statement about what you reported and what they said and give them a copy.

Do not tell the owner about your picture or about the employee's statement. Protect yourself and your business.

Keep your mobile detailing equipment area clean. Your vehicle and the detailing equipment are the first things the clients see. It should be cleaned every night when you return home and detailed once a week.

When your client picks- up their car or you drop it off, make sure you thank them for their service.

Let them know how much you enjoyed detailing their vehicle. Three days later, mail them a thank you letter, letting them know again how much you enjoyed detailing their vehicle and look forward to doing it again. This simple letter will help your future relationship with the client.

People wonder how we are able to keep clients coming back year after, year, after, year. I'm going to tell you the secret of keeping your clients coming back. On every holiday, mail them a card thanking them for their business. On Christmas, we send our clients a box of Christmas cookies and a Christmas card. On Mother's Day, Father's Day, Easter, and the 4th of July, we never forget our clients. If we do this, 90% of our clients always come back.

Sounds simple, doesn't it? Well, try it, my friend. It's worked for me and it will work for you.

One of the most important things to remember when the customers start using your service is to ask them how they heard about you. This simple marketing tool will help you use your advertising dollars more wisely.

You should also ask them, "Who detailed your vehicle before and why is they still them no longer detailing your car?" Use any valuable information gathered as a ways of promoting your business.

Chapter 4

Quickest, Cheapest way to Getting Customers;

Like gas to a fire, clients are the life force to any business. Customers pay your bills, put gas in your car, feed you, and keep your business operating in a professional way. Just like any business, you need customers to stay in business. Not one or two but a steady stream of clients.

Let me tell you how I got my first 10 clients with 25 flyers. In Lexington, Masterson Station Park has an area where people meet with late model restored Mustangs. I walked the area, talking to the Mustang's owners and, handing out flyers. I notice that a completely different group of people came to the parks on the weekend because these were the working families, or retired people, that didn't have the time to detail their vehicle the way it should be done.

I would introduce myself, asking them, "Who waxes, washes, and details your car?" Sometimes, I would talk to several people at the same time. Once we started talking, and I'm getting feedback, I would offer my detailing services 2 times free.

If the customer was using another mobile detailer, I would ask them the following questions;

What are you looking for in a detailing service?

Who details your car?

Are you happy with the service?

How did you find out about the service?

What could this service do better?

How much do they charge?

Do not put down or talk about another mobile detailing business. This is unprofessional. It is wrong and bad business. If the customers have something bad to say about another, listen and take note but do not voice an opinion. If you don't have something nice to say about another man's business, don't say anything.

Keep notes on the customer's replies and use this information to market and improve your mobile detailing business. Always ask them how they heard about the detailing business service. This simple marketing tool will help you advert more wisely.

This is valuable information if you are new to the business. It lets you know what has made the other business successful and what works in that area.

A good marketing system is using what other people say to market your business. If I talk with 18 clients who say, "We love Kelly's Auto Detailing because he uses that new Turtle Shield Wax," when I talk with my next customers, I say; "At Detailers Express, we use Turtle Shield Wax." You can learn a lot from talking with people at this car show, and you may also pick- up new customers.

That's why we ask the clients about their detailer. If a client is looking for another car detailer, we ask them. "Weren't you happy with the service of Kelly's Auto Detailing?" I heard they have a good system."

"No, he smoked while detailing and my car smelled like cigarettes. It took me a month to get the smell out."

"Pete, at Detailing Express, we have a smoke free team who will take care of your car's detailing needs."

Talk to your customers, learn what they like and dislike about the other mobile detailing services, and then think how you can better your service.

Pricing your service is also very simple, if you

know what to do. Talk to your customers to find out how much the other services are charging. You can also call or walk-in their place of business and ask. We don't believe in low bidding just to get clients. But we believe in a fare bid. If the going rate is $45 to $70 a week, I would charge $60 for my service.

We offer 1 free external car wash to anyone who signs up for bi-monthly detailing service. Free is one of the strongest words in the business industry. By offering something or anything free, you will opens the door just wide enough to get your feet in. Even in the hardest markets.

Take before and after pictures of every car you

detail. If you are new to the business, this gives you visual proof of your skills in auto detailing. It also provides you with the opportunity to master your craft. Remember what they say! Practices makes perfect.

If you don't have any money to start your mobile detailing business, there's other ways that you can get clients within the next 7 days, using the people you know. This way is simple but very successful and people are using it every day.

Sit down and make a list of everyone you know. Make list family members, friends, and neighbors, and their landlords or property managers and acquaintances. You need their addresses and phone numbers.

Start with your family and friends. You can call them, but I think it's better to talk with them face-to-face. Let everyone know you are starting a vehicle detailing business and ask for help.

What you are trying to do is get a list of car owners who would like a free car wash. All car owners need their vehicle detailed; people just don't have the time, so it's better to hire someone you know than to bring a stranger to your home to detail your car.

Talk with your spouse; and make a list of all the people she knows. People she works with, church members, gym members, and acquaintances.

Acquaintances are people like your doctor, dentist, mailman, landlord, and veterinarian. Talk with your children and get the names of their teachers, their best friend's parents, and school bus driver.

You can keep your list growing by asking family, friends, neighbors, and acquaintances to fill-out a list of everyone they know. Let people know that this information is very important and you'll need it as soon as possible.

What I did is call everyone on my list and invited them to a chili dinner. Who doesn't love chili? It's cheap to make and most people will not turn down a free meal. Over 35 people showed up, and I told them about my mobile detailing business and, asking them to write down everyone who owned cars before leaving my home. To my amazement, I picked up 5 customers and a list of 92 car owners.

I also made a special offer to the people I invited to the chili dinner. If anyone on their list used my service, we would give them 2 free car washes.

One guy called his uncle, who owned a car leasing business and was looking for a mobile detailer. The next day, I sat down with the guy and we came up with a fair agreement. I would take care of all his cars detailing for $22 per car and my day of service would be on Wednesday. He was the owner of 37 cars and his nephew received a free car wash for a year.

He also agreed to buy all the wax and I could use his building to detail any of my customer's cars.

Let's look at it this way. My investment was $35.00 for the business license, and $60.00 for the chili. This one account turns out to be a $20,000 per year account. Not bad, not bad at all.

For the next 2 weeks, I worked the list, mailing out letters and phone calls, pulling in 12 more clients.

17 customers

New Customers $32 per hour

Estimate 1st 3 Weeks Income $650

Every client is a walking advertisement. Your clients can get you customers quicker than any T.V. or Radio advertisement. Once I had established myself, I made the following offer to my clients, 2 free car washing services for every new customer referred to me. That word "Free" worked its magic, pulling in 5 new customers in 2 weeks.

You can use this same offer to turn your mobile detailing service into a 6 figure yearly income. It works better for people with a big family or a lot of friends. The more people they know, the longer your mailing list. The longer your mailing list, the more customers you will get.

If you are trying to start the detailing business but you have no start-up money and have bad credit, then you must put together a money making plan that will help you to get your business started without investing any money. You can start a detailing business without money, but it will require some work and the help of friends and family.

Offer to pay cash for each new customer who is sent to you by friends, neighbors, and family. You should use a cash offer that will not take too much of your profit. A fair amount to offer is $20 per new customer, if profits from the business allow. Explain that as soon as the customer pays you, you will pay for the referral.

Make a flyer on your computer and print out copies to hand out to people in the neighborhood, friends, family members, and anyone you meet who expresses an interest in your business.

I offered 2 free car washing services to my friends, neighbors, or family for every new customer referred to me. I made the same offer to new customers, 2 free car washing service for every new customer referred to me.

Rent-A-Center made tons on money using this same system on their rentals. Offering their customers half off their next payment, or the next payments free, for every new customer referred to them. Now, banks are using it. My bank pays their customer $50.00 for every new account they referred to them. It is simple. It's a way to get customers without investing any money and it works.

Get Mother to have a Bake Sell:

People love cookies, cakes, pies, and cupcakes, and are willing to pay a little more money for cookies they didn't have to make themselves. Because cupcakes are inexpensive, easy, and quick to make, they are an ideal business start-up project. Get together with your friends, family members, and neighbors to hold a mobile detailing business fundraiser. You might be surprised by how much money you can earn for your business start-up capital. I have a friend who started an office cleaning business using this idea three years ago and now am earning over $300,000.00 a year.

You need to set the time and date for your fundraiser. Because cupcakes are good if the weather is cold or hot, they can be held at any time of year, but mother and grandmother needs to know ahead of time to giving them enough time to make their worlds famous chocolate chips cookies.

My mother and girlfriend had spent three days baking cookies for my detailing fundraiser. We went to the Dollar Tree and purchased several boxes of freezer bags and I stuffed them with cookies. I talked to the manager of a local Kroger and asked him about setting up on the sidewalk outside the entrance. He asked what it was for and I said, "A fundraiser." I offered him a dozen of my mother's world-famous chocolate chip cookies and with a smile, he agreed.

Set your prices. The last time we paid for a dozen of cookies from Sam's Club, it cost me $6.50. We a dozen homemade cookies for $10.00 and sold out. We earn over $800.00 dollars in 4 hours. We all agreed with splitting up the money. $150.00 for my mother, $150.00 for my girlfriend, and $500.00 for my detailing business. That was how a broke man started his detailing service.

Ask current clients if you can post a company sign in their yard as you detail their vehicle, and see if they will allow you to leave it there for a couple days after you complete the job. Offer a promotional discount to those who allow you to advertise your business this way.

If you do a great job with each and every client, they will recommend you to their friends. Make follow-up calls after a job is completed to see that clients are satisfied with your work. Ask them to refer you to friends and family. This is another good way to get started in this business with no money, and free advertisement, is let your work talk for you. Do a thorough job and pay close attention to details. Be meticulous so you do not overlook anything that needs fixing.

Do a walk through with your customer. The most important parts of this business are to make sure your customer is pleased with your service.

How about a local fish fry? If you like to fish or have a friend who's a fisherman, people love fried fish. You could charge up to $5.00 for a fish sandwich and $8.00 for a plate. You can get some baked beans and coleslaw for the plate or meal.

I had a cousin who opened a Lawn Care Service. He didn't have any money, car, lawn mower, trimmer, or blower. After selling fish every Friday and Saturday for 2 months, he was able to get all the equipment needed to start his business.

Chili worked for me. On a cool fall weekend,

Saturday and Sunday after church, there's nothing better than a hot bowl of chili or soup.

The best way to advertise your chili, fish fry, or any food sale is churches and word of mouth. Make some flyers with "Fish Fry" or "Hot Chili" at the top, with your name, phone number, times, and dates on the bottom. Passing out the flyers in your neighborhood or placing those on cars at local churches should get a lot of business. If you ask a week or two before the before the date of the sale, some churches may announce your sale to their members. This will work better if you offer to donate 10 to 15% of the profits to the church.

Make a list of everyone you know, and tell them about your food sale. Don't forget to tell them you're trying to earn money to start-up a detailing business. Most true friends will want to help you so the more people who knows what you are trying to do, the better for your business. Ask them to call and tell everyone they know and ask them to do the same.

42.

HOT CHILI

SALE

FOR CAR DETAILING BUSINESS

START-UP CAPITAL

PLEASE HELP!

438 RACE STREET

1 PM- TO- 7PM

FIRDAY, SATURDAY, & SUNDAY

DATE:

Vegetable Soup

Chicken Noodle

Soup (Sale)

FOR CAR DETAILING BUSINESS

START-UP CAPITAL

PLEASE HELP!

438 RACE STREET

1 PM- TO- 7PM

FIRDAY, SATURDAY, & SUNDAY

DATE:

FRIED FISH

SALE

FOR CAR DETAILING BUSINESS

START-UP CAPITAL

PLEASE HELP!

438 RACE STREET

1 PM- TO- 7PM

FIRDAY, SATURDAY, & SUNDAY

DATE:

45.

SWEET BAKE GOODS

SALE

FOR CAR DETAILING BUSINESS

START-UP CAPITAL

PLEASE HELP!

438 RACE STREET

1 PM- TO- 7PM

FIRDAY, SATURDAY, & SUNDAY

DATE:

Chapter 5

How to find the best customers fast;

We offers on-site detailing for motorcycles, 18-wheelers, tractor trailers, utility trailers, heavy duty equipment, buses, airplanes, helicopters, boats, RVs, and anything on wheels.

Our clients list:

Residents

Auto Dealers- New & Used

Automobile Renting & Leasing Companies

Limousines Services

Motorcycles Dealers

Boat Dealers

Trucking Companies

RV Dealers

RV Renting & Leasing

How to Build Your Detailing Business with Flyers:

Homemade flyers are a great way to promote both large and small detailing services. It's possible to design a flyer on your home computer or by having one created for a small fee by a local printing company. Regardless of how the flyer is made, they all serve the same purpose, which is marketing, for your detailing business.

Local businesses, such as the local grocery store or hardware shop, will generally have a board for local advertising. Any business is free to hang their flyer or business card on these designated areas.

Passing them out in a neighborhood is a great way to get flyers into a customer's hands. First, check with their local laws as some areas do not allow this form of marketing. However, for those that do, handing out flyers at places such as the fair in town, the food court in the mall, or at a flea market are just a few suggestions where how one might use a flyer.

You need to pass out flyers to everyone you think might be interested. Be sure you approach pedestrians in a public area and that you don't block anyone's way. Don't be afraid to approach people, as they're probably shyer about getting the flyer than you are about handing it out. Answer any questions about the information presented on your flyer. Be friendly and smile because you could be talking to a future customer.

I would not leave flyers off on doorsteps because someone may slip on it and fall. Put in mail slots if your flyer is applicable to the area. This is a good approach for advertising your detailing business.

Keep up your distribution efforts for as long as possible. You might reach someone you didn't the first time. If your flyer is torn down or removed, put a new one up. I found out years ago that persistence pays off.

Years ago, after I was discharged from the service, I read a book called, How to Start a Delivery Service. It was a little 50 page paperback loaded with tons of information. On the section about promoting your business, it had information that I still use today. He called it flooding your market and this is how it works.

This is a trick to pulling in customers in the same area, cutting your cost in gas from this area to another. Plus, when a customer sees your business name in their faces three or four times a month, when it is time to wash the cars, they think about you.

This little secret technique has always worked over the years. I call it working an area. If you are dropping off flyers door-to-door or mailing your flyers to a mailing list, work your list until your clients call you and tell you to stop dropping off your flyers.

You see proof that this system works every week. Think about it. How many times do you get fast food, automobile oil change, and department store coupons every month? Even if you never go to that store, restaurant, or oil change service, once or twice a month, every month, you receive the same ads from the same companies. These companies are spending thousands of dollars every month, month after month, year after year.

Why? Because it works, and it will work for you, believe me. I tested it and it will make you money.

Dropping your business flyers at a front door or tucked in a screen is legal unless the homeowner or resident has posted a "no solicitation" or "no distribution" sign. If a property owner/resident has ordered a flyer distributor off his property and the person comes back, the police may be called, and fines, trespassing charges, or other criminal charges may result. But if you see any flyers or door hangers on the door, it is safe.

The easy way to make effective flyers:

What kind of paper should you use? When picking the paper for your flyers, which you can find at any copy shop, such as Quick Print, Copy Express, or Office Max, decide on a color, preferably something that will stand out so people will remember the flyer.

Start off with something at the top of your flyer that will capture your customer's attention. How about "First Detailing 50% off For the First 20

Customers Who Calls." You can have the coupon at the top to grab people's interest. Add an incentive for keeping the flyer, such as a, "$25.00 Complete Auto Detailing for the First 30 People Who Calls." If you are making this offer, your phone will be ringing off the hook. I have had customers calling me at 5 o'clock in the morning, wanting to know if the offer is still good.

This is how it works. When the customer calls you, respond to the call as soon as possible. Be on time; and do your best job and when you've completed detailing their car, gives them your business card.

You know what services they want and how long it takes to detail their car. What I say to them is, "Thank you for using our service. When would you like your next detail service?" You will be amazed by how well this works.

According to the Direct Marketing Association, flyers and door hanger's response rates are usually between 1 and 3 percent.

That means you should get one or three phone calls out of every 100 flyers you put out, if your flyer looks good and catch your customer's attention. But by adding, (Call today and we will detail your car for

$25.00; No Obligation) on my flyers', my response jumped to 6 to 8 percent. Call for 50% off on your first detailing, or (Call today and we will detail your car for only $25.00). Six customers responded, and out of the six, four called back for the complete service two months later.

But in order to get my phone ringing faster, I added this: (This offer is only available to the first 20 Customers, please be the first to call "[your number")]. This works, trust me. You will get so many clients; you will not know what to do with them. This simple little technique will give you all the business you need.

What do I do when the phone starts ringing? I give this offer to everyone and. I do not care if they are number 25. If it is possible for us to detail to 25 vehicles in the next few days, I am there, doing my best to make that client happy.

I know what you're thinking; if I make this offer, I am going to get ripped off. The truth is that most people will not rip you off. Yes, some may not become regular clients, but more will. The best part about this offer is most detailing services will not make this offer; which will open the door for you.

Save Money By Using Door Hangers:

What are door hangers? They are rectangular in shape and are longer than they are wide. They have a circular hole near the top to slide them onto a doorknob. Each door hanger contains a message for the customer, with information about your detailing service. This message can be a special offer for services in their neighborhood. Sometimes, door hangers are used for decoration.

I use more door hangers the flyers to advertise my detailing business. Have door hangers made with your business logo, company name, and contact information. Hand them out or pay to have various hotels or restaurants give them out to their customers.

Put out 600 door hangers in a chosen area once a week for the next ten weeks. Ten weeks putting out-door hangers- on the same doors, over and over again.

Your response rate will be amazing, cutting your gas rate down, and raising your profits ratio, putting more money in your pockets.

My door hangers had a big title that said, "Call us today and we will detail your car for only $25.00, if you are the first of 20 customers to call (No Obligations)" along with an eye-catching and dramatic color photo. We found this little wording on door hangers caused folks to at least check the body of the message.

How to Make Door Hanger At Home:

By using your computer or a friend's computer, you can make your own door hangers from home. This is what I do.

Go into All Programs and select a word processing program such as Microsoft Office, Microsoft Word, or Open Office Writer. Click on the "format" tab and select "columns". Choose a minimum of three columns and click "ok".

Change your page layout to land-scape by clicking on the "file" and selecting "page set-up". Choose "land-scape" and click "ok".

Next, you can begin designing your door hanger flyers. You will be able to fit three on a page, one per column. Make sure to include your contact information and the name of your product and service, and your attention catching offers. Attention grabbing offer goes across the top of the page in bold print. This should be the first thing your customers see.

Next, you should print out your first draft and ask some family members or neighbors for their opinions. Have them check for spelling errors, typos, and errors in consistency. Have them make suggestions on how to improve your flyer. Make any suggested changes and have your proofreaders check the flyer one last time.

If you decide to use black and white photos or no photos at all, and then it is fine to print your flyers in black and white.

The first printing of new detailing service flyers should be small, 300 or 500 are enough. Hand these out and measure your response rate by keeping track of who calls. You may decide to do this with a special offer that you have only advertised on your flyers. Like; (: Call us today and we will detail your vehicle for $25.00.)

We put out a ton of flyers and door hangers each week. The best way to do it is to hire a couple kids and pay them by the flyer. Paying them 4 cents per flyer and it makes them work faster.

You can also contact the area newspaper

distributor and ask him to include your flyer in his distribution along with newspaper. They have fixed rates generally.

Flyer Delivery Service,

These companies are professional and looking for long-term customers. I look for the service that has that has been in business for ten years or longer. I also ask for reference. They will professionally design your flyers and deliver them for a fee.

Chapter 6

How to keep customers happy:

You've written a sales letter that you think is going to knock their socks off. (See if you haven't yet.) Before mailing it out, have a look at these sales letters tips to make ensure you're maximizing the return on your sales letter campaign.

Mail Your Sales Letter To The Right People:

If the intent of your sales letter is to detail vehicles, for example, you want to send it just to car owners in your area, not to people who don't own a car. Even though the best mailing list is one that you've built personally from your own prospect list, we use the yellow pages to focus your sales letter campaign on specific categories of potential customers. You can also buy mailing lists from mailing list brokers.

All your customers or clients are not the same. So why should you expect them all to be persuaded by exactly the same sales letter? Create different versions of your sales letter for different segments of your target market by emphasizing different benefits of your offer or by changing the benefits completely.

Writing the name and address of the recipient directly onto the envelope will increase your sales letter response. Also, direct marketing studies have shown that having names and addresses handwritten is the surest way to get your sales letter opened. However, this may not be appropriate for your business image.

Get a ton of business by re-mailing 2 or 3 weeks later.

If you've forgotten everything else in this book, remember this: sending out another mailing to the same list should get a response of about half the original response. Not bad at all when the work is already done!

Besides sending your sales letter to prospective customers through the mail, you might also use email. However, be aware that people generally are more receptive to unsolicited mail arriving through the mail than to unsolicited email.

In the next few pages, you will find some of the most successful sales letters we used to turn our business from a small, two man operation to over $150,000.00 a year, detailing car dealerships.

We began with door hanger and weeks later, decided onto mailing them out.

First, we put together a mailing list. We used the local yellow pages to get the names and addresses of, auto dealerships, vehicle leasing services, motorcycles dealerships, and limousines services, in every town within 50 miles of our business.

Re-mailing is the secret to success in this business. Once we had our mailing list of over 400 companies, we mailed out the first sales letter to the first 100 customers on a Sunday night. A week later, we mail out the same letter to the next 100. We did this once a week for a month.

We followed up with the second sales letter the following month and the next letter the following month.

What was our response ratio? Let me put it this way. Within three months, we had 6 car dealerships, 2 limousines services, 2 motorcycles dealerships and 4 auto leasing companies, which is enough work to keep 4 full-time employees busy five days a week.

One the next page, you will find our rate sheet. This is based on the rates we charge for those dealerships.

But you can call other detailers in your area to set your price.

Make sure to mail a copy of your price list along with all your sales letters.

Best prices to charge for your service;

My rates are based on rates in my area in Central Kentucky. We came up with these prices after talking with customers and other mobile detailing services. Before you price your services, talk to detailers and customers in your area.

Exterior Washing- $15

Exterior Wash, Hand Dry, Tire Dressing, Outside Windows!

Exterior & Interior Clean- $20

Exterior Wash, Hand Dry, Tire Dressing, Outside &

Inside Windows, Vacuum Seats & Carpets, and Dashboard & Vinyl Cleaning!

Exterior & Interior Clean with Floor Mats- $30

Shampooing with same service as number 2, including floor Mats!

Exterior Wash & Wax- $40

Exterior Wash, Wax, Hand Dry, and Tire Dressing

Premium Clean- $50

Exterior Wash, Hand Dry, Tire Dressing, Outside &

Inside Windows, Vacuum Seats & Carpets, and Dashboard & Vinyl Cleaning Armorial!

Super Detail- $65

Exterior & Interior Wash, Wax, and Shampoo!

Full Detail- $85

Engine Detail, Exterior & Interior Detail, Wax, Shampoo, Carpets, Meats, Trunk Detail, Armorial, Vacuum, Clay Bar, Tire Dressing, and Leather Conditioning!

Craft's Mobile Detailing

Let Us Detail "Your Vehicle!"

Exterior Washing- $15

Exterior Wash, Hand Dry, Tire Dressing, Outside Windows!

Exterior & Interior Clean- $20

Exterior Wash, Hand Dry, Tire Dressing, Outside & Inside Windows, Vacuum Seats & Carpets, and Dashboard & Vinyl Cleaning!

Exterior & Interior Clean with Floor Mats- $30

Shampooing with same service as number 2, including floor mats!

Exterior Wash & Wax- $40

Exterior Wash, Wax, Hand Dry, and Tire Dressing

Premium Clean- $50

Exterior Wash, Hand Dry, Tire Dressing, Outside & Inside Windows, Vacuum Seats & Carpets, and Dashboard & Vinyl Cleaning Armorial!

Super Detail- $65

Exterior & Interior Wash, Wax, and Shampoo!

Craft's Mobile Detailing

We'll come to You Mobile Detailing!

Exterior Washing- $15

Exterior Wash, Hand Dry, Tire Dressing, Outside Windows!

Exterior & Interior Clean- $20

Exterior Wash, Hand Dry, Tire Dressing, Outside & Inside Windows, Vacuum Seats & Carpets, and Dashboard & Vinyl Cleaning!

Exterior & Interior Clean with Floor Mats- $30

Shampooing with same service as number 2, including floor mats!

Exterior Wash & Wax- $40

Exterior Wash, Wax, Hand Dry, and Tire Dressing

Premium Clean- $50

Exterior Wash, Hand Dry, Tire Dressing, Outside & Inside Windows, Vacuum Seats & Carpets, and Dashboard & Vinyl Cleaning Armorial!

Craft's Mobile Detailing

Is your vehicle dirty? No time to wash it? Let Craft's

Mobile Detailing cleans your vehicle for you!

Exterior Washing- $15

Exterior Wash, Hand Dry, Tire Dressing, Outside Windows!

Exterior & Interior Clean- $20

Exterior Wash, Hand Dry, Tire Dressing, Outside & Inside Windows, Vacuum Seats & Carpets, and Dashboard & Vinyl Cleaning!

Exterior & Interior Clean with Floor Mats- $30

Shampooing with same service as number 2, including floor mats!

Exterior Wash & Wax- $40

Exterior Wash, Wax, Hand Dry, and Tire Dressing

Premium Clean- $50

Exterior Wash, Hand Dry, Tire Dressing, Outside & Inside Windows, Vacuum Seats & Carpets, and Dashboard & Vinyl Cleaning Armorial!

Craft's Mobile Detailing

Looking for a complete exterior & interior detailer? Nothing is overlooked; we'll clean your vehicle from top to bottom!

Exterior Washing- $15

Exterior Wash, Hand Dry, Tire Dressing, Outside Windows!

Exterior & Interior Clean- $20

Exterior Wash, Hand Dry, Tire Dressing, Outside & Inside Windows, Vacuum Seats & Carpets, and Dashboard & Vinyl Cleaning!

Exterior & Interior Clean with Floor Mats- $30

Shampooing with same service as number 2, including floor mats!

Exterior Wash & Wax- $40

Exterior Wash, Wax, Hand Dry, and Tire Dressing

Premium Clean- $50

Exterior Wash, Hand Dry, Tire Dressing, Outside & Inside Windows, Vacuum Seats & Carpets, and Dashboard & Vinyl Cleaning Armorial!

Super Detail- $65

Exterior & Interior Wash, Wax, and Shampoo!

Craft's Mobile Detailing

We offer top detailing service, done by skilled, experienced personnel and at very competitive prices!

Exterior Washing- $15

Exterior Wash, Hand Dry, Tire Dressing, Outside Windows!

Exterior & Interior Clean- $20

Exterior Wash, Hand Dry, Tire Dressing, Outside & Inside Windows, Vacuum Seats & Carpets, and Dashboard & Vinyl Cleaning!

Exterior & Interior Clean with Floor Mats- $30

Shampooing with same service as number 2, including floor mats!

Exterior Wash & Wax- $40

Exterior Wash, Wax, Hand Dry, and Tire Dressing

Premium Clean- $50

Exterior Wash, Hand Dry, Tire Dressing, Outside & Inside Windows, Vacuum Seats & Carpets, and Dashboard & Vinyl Cleaning Armorial!

Super Detail- $65

Exterior & Interior Wash, Wax, and Shampoo!

Craft's Mobile Detailing

Once we're finished with your vehicle, people

Will think it just came out of the showroom!

Exterior Washing- $15

Exterior Wash, Hand Dry, Tire Dressing, Outside Windows!

Exterior & Interior Clean- $20

Exterior Wash, Hand Dry, Tire Dressing, Outside & Inside Windows, Vacuum Seats & Carpets, and Dashboard & Vinyl Cleaning!

Exterior & Interior Clean with Floor Mats- $30

Shampooing with same service as number 2, including floor mats!

Exterior Wash & Wax- $40

Exterior Wash, Wax, Hand Dry, and Tire Dressing

Premium Clean- $50

Exterior Wash, Hand Dry, Tire Dressing, Outside & Inside Windows, Vacuum Seats & Carpets, and Dashboard & Vinyl Cleaning Armorial!

Super Detail- $65

Exterior & Interior Wash, Wax, and Shampoo!

Craft's Mobile Detailing

Is dirt, grime, bird poop, and pollution infested your vehicle? Flight back with the best detailer in town!

Exterior Washing- $15

Exterior Wash, Hand Dry, Tire Dressing, Outside Windows!

Exterior & Interior Clean- $20

Exterior Wash, Hand Dry, Tire Dressing, Outside & Inside Windows, Vacuum Seats & Carpets, and Dashboard & Vinyl Cleaning!

Exterior & Interior Clean with Floor Mats- $30

Shampooing with same service as number 2, including floor mats!

Exterior Wash & Wax- $40

Exterior Wash, Wax, Hand Dry, and Tire Dressing

Premium Clean- $50

Exterior Wash, Hand Dry, Tire Dressing, Outside & Inside Windows, Vacuum Seats & Carpets, and Dashboard & Vinyl Cleaning Armorial!

Super Detail- $65

Exterior & Interior Wash, Wax, and Shampoo!

Craft's Mobile Detailing

Make an appointment with one of our experts to care for your vehicle's detailing needs. We'll make your rider look new!

Exterior Washing- $15

Exterior Wash, Hand Dry, Tire Dressing, Outside Windows!

Exterior & Interior Clean- $20

Exterior Wash, Hand Dry, Tire Dressing, Outside & Inside Windows, Vacuum Seats & Carpets, and Dashboard & Vinyl Cleaning!

Exterior & Interior Clean with Floor Mats- $30

Shampooing with same service as number 2, including floor mats!

Exterior Wash & Wax- $40

Exterior Wash, Wax, Hand Dry, and Tire Dressing

Premium Clean- $50

Exterior Wash, Hand Dry, Tire Dressing, Outside & Inside Windows, Vacuum Seats & Carpets, and Dashboard & Vinyl Cleaning Armorial!

Super Detail- $65

Exterior & Interior Wash, Wax, and Shampoo!

Craft's Mobile Detailing

At Craft's Mobile Detailing, we make cars look brand new again!

Exterior Washing- $15

Exterior Wash, Hand Dry, Tire Dressing, Outside Windows!

Exterior & Interior Clean- $20

Exterior Wash, Hand Dry, Tire Dressing, Outside & Inside Windows, Vacuum Seats & Carpets, and Dashboard & Vinyl Cleaning!

Exterior & Interior Clean with Floor Mats- $30

Exterior Wash & Wax- $40

Exterior Wash, Wax, Hand Dry, and Tire Dressing

Premium Clean- $50

Exterior Wash, Hand Dry, Tire Dressing, Outside & Inside Windows, Vacuum Seats & Carpets, and Dashboard & Vinyl Cleaning Armorial!

Super Detail- $65

Exterior & Interior Wash, Wax, and Shampoo!

Craft's Mobile Detailing

We offer a first class detailing. Excellent prices Guaranteed!

Exterior Washing- $15

Exterior Wash, Hand Dry, Tire Dressing, Outside Windows!

Exterior & Interior Clean- $20

Exterior Wash, Hand Dry, Tire Dressing, Outside & Inside Windows, Vacuum Seats & Carpets, and Dashboard & Vinyl Cleaning!

Exterior & Interior Clean with Floor Mats- $30

Shampooing with same service as number 2, including floor mats!

Exterior Wash & Wax- $40

Exterior Wash, Wax, Hand Dry, and Tire Dressing

Premium Clean- $50

Exterior Wash, Hand Dry, Tire Dressing, Outside & Inside Windows, Vacuum Seats & Carpets, and Dashboard & Vinyl Cleaning Armorial!

Super Detail- $65

Exterior & Interior Wash, Wax, and Shampoo!

Craft's Mobile Detailing

 Give your vehicle that new look, smell, and feeling back again. We are a mobile detailer; if you can't come to us, we'll come to you!

Exterior Washing- $15

Exterior Wash, Hand Dry, Tire Dressing, Outside Windows!

Exterior & Interior Clean- $20

Exterior Wash, Hand Dry, Tire Dressing, Outside & Inside Windows, Vacuum Seats & Carpets, and Dashboard & Vinyl Cleaning!

Exterior & Interior Clean with Floor Mats- $30

Shampooing with same service as number 2, including floor mats!

Exterior Wash & Wax- $40

Exterior Wash, Wax, Hand Dry, and Tire Dressing

Premium Clean- $50

Exterior Wash, Hand Dry, Tire Dressing, Outside & Inside Windows, Vacuum Seats & Carpets, and Dashboard & Vinyl Cleaning Armorial!

Super Detail- $65

Exterior & Interior Wash, Wax, and Shampoo!

Craft's Mobile Detailing

Craft's Mobile Detailing is the #1 name in high quality, on-site automotive detailing. We offer all of the same detail services of a high-end detail shop, but at your location, for your convenience.

Exterior Washing- $15

Exterior Wash, Hand Dry, Tire Dressing, Outside Windows!

Exterior & Interior Clean- $20

Exterior Wash, Hand Dry, Tire Dressing, Outside & Inside Windows, Vacuum Seats & Carpets, and Dashboard & Vinyl Cleaning!

Exterior & Interior Clean with Floor Mats- $30

Shampooing with same service as number 2, including floor mats!

Exterior Wash & Wax- $40

Exterior Wash, Wax, Hand Dry, and Tire Dressing

Premium Clean- $50

Exterior Wash, Hand Dry, Tire Dressing, Outside & Inside Windows, Vacuum Seats & Carpets, and Dashboard & Vinyl Cleaning Armorial!

Craft's Mobile Detailing

Make your vehicle look professional and slick. We invite you to get the "best detailing in the state!"

Exterior Washing- $15

Exterior Wash, Hand Dry, Tire Dressing, Outside Windows!

Exterior & Interior Clean- $20

Exterior Wash, Hand Dry, Tire Dressing, Outside & Inside Windows, Vacuum Seats & Carpets, and Dashboard & Vinyl Cleaning!

Exterior & Interior Clean with Floor Mats- $30

Shampooing with same service as number 2, including floor mats!

Exterior Wash & Wax- $40

Exterior Wash, Wax, Hand Dry, and Tire Dressing

Premium Clean- $50

Exterior Wash, Hand Dry, Tire Dressing, Outside & Inside Windows, Vacuum Seats & Carpets, and Dashboard & Vinyl Cleaning Armorial!

Super Detail- $65   Exterior & Interior Wash, Wax, and Shampoo!

Craft's Mobile Detailing

With over 10 years' experience in auto detailing, we look forward to making your vehicle look new again.

Exterior Washing- $15

Exterior Wash, Hand Dry, Tire Dressing, Outside Windows!

Exterior & Interior Clean- $20

Exterior Wash, Hand Dry, Tire Dressing, Outside & Inside Windows, Vacuum Seats & Carpets, and Dashboard & Vinyl Cleaning!

Exterior & Interior Clean with Floor Mats- $30

Shampooing with same service as number 2, including floor mats!

Exterior Wash & Wax- $40

Exterior Wash, Wax, Hand Dry, and Tire Dressing

Premium Clean- $50

Exterior Wash, Hand Dry, Tire Dressing, Outside & Inside Windows, Vacuum Seats & Carpets, and Dashboard & Vinyl Cleaning Armorial!

Super Detail- $65 Exterior & Interior Wash, Wax, and Shampoo!

Craft's Mobile Detailing

Professional quality detailing service, any make or model. No job too big, no job too small for our personal care!

Exterior Washing- $15

Exterior Wash, Hand Dry, Tire Dressing, Outside Windows!

Exterior & Interior Clean- $20

Exterior Wash, Hand Dry, Tire Dressing, Outside & Inside Windows, Vacuum Seats & Carpets, and Dashboard & Vinyl Cleaning!

Exterior & Interior Clean with Floor Mats- $30

Shampooing with same service as number 2, including floor mats!

Exterior Wash & Wax- $40

Exterior Wash, Wax, Hand Dry, and Tire Dressing

Premium Clean- $50

Exterior Wash, Hand Dry, Tire Dressing, Outside & Inside Windows, Vacuum Seats & Carpets, and Dashboard & Vinyl Cleaning Armorial!

Super Wax, and Detail- $65 Exterior & Interior Wash, Shampoo!

Chapter 11

A very simple, but highly effective way to control your money:

Warning, warning, warning! Do not try to get too big too fast. I made that mistake once in this business, using the multi-mailing, and continuing putting out flyers. New accounts were ringing the phone off the hook, and the only thing I saw was dollars. I was too much into to making money and was not thinking about running my business. I ended in trouble with the IRS and almost lost everything.

This is a business. When money is coming in hand over fist, we make the mistake of thinking, that "I am going enjoy myself," going out purchasing a new pick-up truck and 20 employees and. And the next thing you know, reality hits and we are in trouble.

My simple bookkeeping system, which that has worked for me for years, is called the 1/3 payroll system. This way, everyone gets paid. This is how it works. My rate for detailing a car is $125.00 a vehicle, I pay myself $45.00. I pay my company $40.00 and I pay my employees $40.00 per unit.

But the trick making this work for your business is to leave the money were it is at. The purpose for paying yourself is living, buying your food, paying your bills, and surviving. The money you pay into your business is for equipment, advertising, and gas. This money keeps your business going year after year. The money for employees can be used in two different ways.

During the slow times, you still need to pay your bills. I start planning for the slow days with the first detailing. That is why when you start; you should try to do most of the work yourself. If you go out and earn $300.00 in one day detailing cars or whatever, does not take your wife or girlfriend out that night and blow $300.00 on a night in town. That is just stupid.

What I would do with the $300.00 is pay myself $100.00 and the remaining $200.00 goes in savings in your business account. If you follow this same simple bookkeeping system, and do not touch the money in your business and employee account, your business will continue to grow every year.

This is what my bookkeeping notes look like:

March 1/2010

- 4 Details
- Earned Income $500.00
- Company's Income   - $168.00

- Employee's Income   - $166.00

- Owner's Gross Income   - $166.00

- Bal. Owner's Net   - $83.00

- Slow Days   - $83.00

On the business income, use it for mainly advertising during your first year. I would not buy any new equipment because you are trying to build your business account up for the following season. If you have a car and cell phone, if you do not have a car and cannot borrow one, I would check auto auctions or go to an auto repair shop and buy me a low-cost, low mileage automobile or truck.

Remember, we are trying to build a business, not go down the first year.

On employee income, I would not hire any employees unless I get reach a point where it is impossible for me to handle the work, and I would hire only a part-time employee.

Before I hired my first employee, I was detailing 2 to 5 units a day, five days a week and my wife was answering the phone.

If you make it through the first year and do not have to hire any employees, that is great. But if you follow the steps in this book, one will need help. Every time you detail a vehicle, takes out your employee payroll and one must manage one's money carefully.

If you detailing business grow bigger, also your income will as well. Here is an example: Let's say you're detailing 4 cars a day, and charging you're customers $125.00 per unit.

April 1, 2010

- Cars 4 Xx $125.00 = $500.00 Xx 5 days = $2,500.00

- Weekly   Earned   Income $2,500.00

- Company's Income $834.00

- Employee's Income $833.00

- Owner's Gross $833.00

- Owner's Net $417.00

- Slow week's pay $416.00

At the end of the month, the money is counted to make sure that it balances with the books. If your income taxes are paid quarterly, you take that money out of your business account. If you are paying it yearly, you would send your money in

February after you're working year, taking the money from your business account. The balance in the business account is put into savings for start-up capital for the following month.

If you have employees, you are stepping on bookkeeper grounds. Finding a good, dependable, low-cost bookkeeper is the way to go. They will handle your employee tax, business, and personal taxes. But if you don't need an employee, save that income for the next year.

Some businesses use self-employed detailers to save them the headaches of employee's taxes, and workmen's comp. insurance. Check your state's laws to ensure you are not breaking any laws. But this is how this changes when using self-employed detailers.

April 1, 2010

- Units 4 Xx $125.00 = $500.00 Xx 5 days = $2,500.00

- Weekly   Earned   Income $2,500.00

- Company's Income $834.00

- Employee's Income $833.00

- Owner's Gross $833.00

- Owner's Net $417.00

- Slow week's pay $416.00

Keep track of your money:

Like the software programs for scheduling, there are programs to help you do your own bookkeeping. My favorite, which makes keeping track of your small business finances easy, even if you can't add or subtract, is outright.com, which is around $10 a month and even reminds you when taxes are due or when you overlook a deduction.

Almost 98% of the people whose businesses go under do not plan ahead. They will work hard earning $300 and go out and blow the money in a few days. You earned the money, I cannot tell you what to do with it. But if you want to stay in the detailing business and earn a good income, follow my system.

Good luck, my friend.

Printed in Great Britain
by Amazon